THE SOLO GIRL'S
Bali
TRAVEL BUCKET LIST

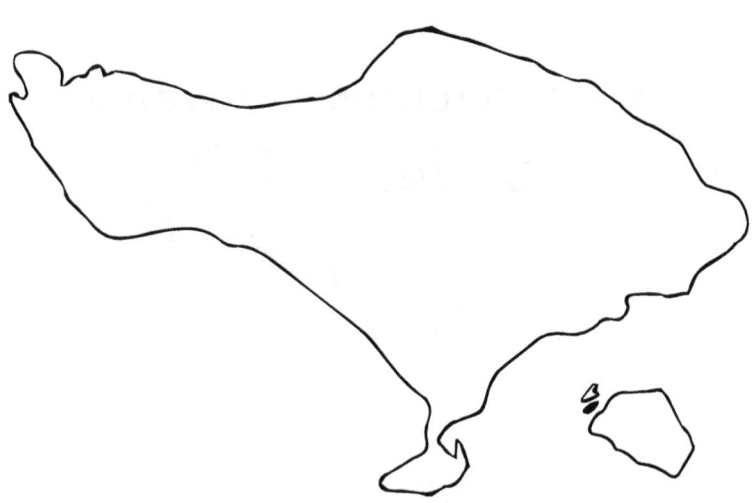

ALEXA WEST GUIDES

WHEN I FOLLOW MY HEART,
I WAKE UP IN... *Bali!*

A dream is just a goal... plus a plan!

This bucket list is yours forever.
Keep track of where you've been.
Make plans for where you're going.

If you're reading this right now, know that you are different. If you're reading this, it means that you dream bigger and feel deeper than most people who live their whole lives in one place.

But just in case you ever think a deam is too big, here's what I want you to remember...

STOP WAITING FOR PERMISSION!

Why do we wait for someone else to give us permission to make big moves?

To take a trip.
To chop our hair off.
To start a YouTube channel, write a book, or create a business.

Because we all have the same fear: What if my light shines too bright?

Is that okay? Am I allowed to be shiny? Am I allowed to sparkle? Am I allowed to change?

Yes. Yes. Yes. And yes.

You are allowed to be all those things...because those things are already you.

Stop playing small.
It doesn't serve you and it doesnt help anyone around you.

Be as bright as you can be, because when your light shines bright - you attract the right people into your life. Shiny people.

When you give yourself permission to live a shiny, sparkly and bright life, you wake up excited in the morning. You stop living in fear. And you inspire the people living in the dark.

So, give yourself permission to do everything you've always wanted to do. Give yourself permission to be the person you've always wanted to be. Starting with this journal...

Remember why you travel...

I travel because...

Travel makes me appreciate...

When I book a ticket I feel...

When I get on a plane, I know...

And when I land in a new place, I can finally....

I'm living a life full of...

I am living my best life!

Who I want to travel with!

#travelBFF

MY PERSONAL
Travel Goals

- [ ] Go scuba diving!
- [ ] _____
- [ ] _____
- [ ] _____
- [ ] _____
- [ ] _____
- [ ] _____
- [ ] _____
- [ ] _____
- [ ] _____
- [ ] _____

travel fears
I WILL CONQUER

- [ ] Travel Solo!
- [ ]
- [ ]
- [ ]
- [ ]
- [ ]
- [ ]
- [ ]
- [ ]
- [ ]
- [ ]
- [ ]
- [ ]
- [ ]

FIRST,
LET'S KEEP TRACK
OF YOUR
Bali adventures!

cities, towns & villages
—to visit!

- [ ] Amed
- [ ] Ubud
- [ ] Canggu
- [ ] Berawa
- [ ] Umalas
- [ ] Seminyak
- [ ] Jimbaran
- [ ] Uluwatu
- [ ] Sidemen
- [ ] Candidasa
- [ ] Sumberkima
- [ ] Pererenan
- [ ] Nusa Lembongan
- [ ] Nusa Ceningan
- [ ] Nusa Penida

add your own!

WHAT OTHER BALI SPOTS HAVE YOU VISITED?

- [ ] _____
- [ ] _____
- [ ] _____
- [ ] _____
- [ ] _____
- [ ] _____
- [ ] _____
- [ ] _____
- [ ] _____
- [ ] _____
- [ ] _____

fun fact!

Bali is the only Hindu Island in Indonesia - which is the most populous muslim country in the world.

Bali

CHALLENGES

- ☐ Learn How To Ride A Scooter
- ☐ Learn To Eat Nasi Campur With Your Hands
- ☐ Memorize At Least 3 Indo Words Or Phrases
- ☐ Meet At Least 3 Wayans
- ☐ Try Sambal Without Crying
- ☐ Eat At a Restaurant By Yourself
- ☐ Eat a Vegan Meal and Like It
- ☐ Discover your Balinese Name (Wayan, Made, Nyoman, Ketut)

fun fact!

80% of Bali's economy is tourism! Bali loves when you visit!

- [ ] Lawar
- [ ] Satay
- [ ] Tempe
- [ ] Gado Gado
- [ ] Nasi Campur
- [ ] Babi Guling
- [ ] Sambal Matah
- [ ] Nasi Goreng
- [ ] Mie Goreng
- [ ] Ketchup Manis (a sweet sauce to put on your Mie Goreng)
- [ ] Smoothie Bowls (okay, that's more of a "Bali" thing but they're good)

drinks to drink!

- [ ] Jamu
- [ ] Bali Kopi
- [ ] Bintang Beer
- [ ] Fresh Mango Juice or Pineapple Juice
- [ ] Arak (just take a tiny sip of this strong alcohol - so you can say you've tried it!)
- [ ] Coconut Water from a Fresh Coconut

fun fact!

You'll meet many Balinese people with the names Wayan, Made, Nyoman or Ketut. These names are given in the order they are born.

famous cafés
TO VISIT

- [ ] The Loft, Canggu
- [ ] Crate Cafe, Canggu
- [ ] Milk n Madu, Ubud
- [ ] Yellow Flower Cafe, Ubud
- [ ] KYND Cafe, Seminyak
- [ ] Bali Bola, Seminyak
- [ ] Tropicana Churros, Umalas
- [ ] Rimba Cafe, Amed
- [ ] Revolver Espresso, Seminyak

best restaurants
TO TRY

- [ ] Merah Putih, Seminyak
- [ ] Warung Nia, Seminyak
- [ ] Motel Mexicola, Seminyak
- [ ] Sangsaka, Seminyak
- [ ] Bikini Restaurant, Seminyak
- [ ] Warung Bu Mi, Canggu
- [ ] Luigis Pizza, Canggu
- [ ] Tacos Aqui, Umalas
- [ ] Synkonah, Berawa
- [ ] Room4Dessert, Ubud
- [ ] Milk N Madu, Ubud
- [ ] Moksa, Ubud
- [ ] Zest, Ubud

beaches to visit!

- [ ] Amed Beach, Amed
- [ ] Virgin Beach, Candidasa
- [ ] Green Bowl Beach, Pecatu
- [ ] Nyang Nyang Beach, Pecatu
- [ ] Suluban Beach, Uluwatu
- [ ] Bingin Beach, Uluwatu
- [ ] Melasti Beach, Uluwatu
- [ ] Batu Belig, Seminyak
- [ ] Petitenget Beach, Seminyak
- [ ] Double Six Beach, Seminyak
- [ ] Echo Beach, Canggu
- [ ] Batu Bolong Beach, Canggu
- [ ] Diamond Beach, Nusa Penida
- [ ] Kelingking Beach, Nusa Penida
- [ ] Tembeling Beach, Nusa Penida
- [ ] Secret Point Beach, Nusa Ceningan

THE BEST
beach clubs

- ☐ Omnia, Uluwatu
- ☐ Karma Beach Club, Uluwatu
- ☐ Sundays Beach Club, Uluwatu
- ☐ Ku De Ta, Seminyak
- ☐ Potato Head, Seminyak
- ☐ Palmilla, Uluwatu
- ☐ Single Finns, Uluwatu
- ☐ Finns, Berawa
- ☐ COMO Beach Club, Canggu
- ☐ The Lawn, Canggu
- ☐ La Brisa, Echo Beach

fun fact!

Balinese people don't really "date around". They date to match and marry.

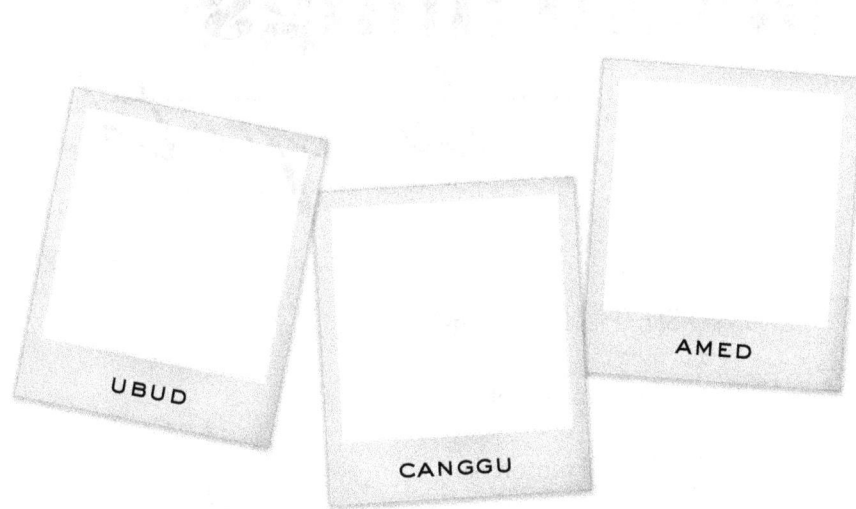

Draw your impressions of...

island things

- [ ] Canang Sari (Hindu blessings)
- [ ] People in cafes...barefoot
- [ ] A family of 4 on 1 motorbike
- [ ] A full grown dog on a motorbike
- [ ] A child under the age of 12 driving a motorbike
- [ ] A Balinese person carrying something outrageous while driving a motorbike (a ladder, a barrel, 8-foot long bamboo)
- [ ] Guys driving motorbikes without a shirt or helmet in Canggu
- [ ] Someone doing free-flow interpretive dance on the beach...alone
- [ ] Balinese women carry baskets of offerings (or tanks of gas) on their head.

transport *to take!*

- [ ] Feet
- [ ] Bicycle
- [ ] Motorbike
- [ ] GoJek Car
- [ ] Surfboard
- [ ] Speed Ferry
- [ ] GoJek Motorbike
- [ ] White Water Raft
- [ ] Back of a Truck
- [ ] Solo Girl's Travel Squad Car
- [ ] Fishing Boat in Amed (Jukong)
- [ ] Buggy (Nusa Lembongan Hotel Transport)

WORDS & PHRASES TO *listen for*

- [ ] Karma
- [ ] Vibe
- [ ] Tribe
- [ ] Flow
- [ ] Woke
- [ ] Mindset
- [ ] Chakras
- [ ] Breathwork
- [ ] Catch Sunset
- [ ] The Shortcut
- [ ] Campur (pronounced Cham-pur)

BALI BASED BOOKS *to read*

- [ ] The Solo Girl's Travel Guide: Bali
- [ ] Eat, Pray, Love (skip the movie, it sucked)
- [ ] Snowing in Bali

animals *to see!*

- [ ] Bats
- [ ] Geckos
- [ ] Monkeys
- [ ] Tiger Fish
- [ ] Angel Fish
- [ ] Giant Ants
- [ ] Sea Turtles
- [ ] Manta Rays
- [ ] Sea Urchins
- [ ] Skink Lizards
- [ ] Mola Mola Fish
- [ ] Banteng (Brown Cows)
- [ ] Water Monitors (Giant Lizards)

pro tip!

Do not visit the zoos, civet coffee plantations or elephant "sanctuaries". These establishments do not comply with animal rights and there are no official sanctuaries on the island. #ResponsibleTourism

top 10 *Bali* EXPERIENCES

- [ ] Surfing
- [ ] Snorkeling
- [ ] Scuba Diving
- [ ] Kecak Fire Dance
- [ ] Waterfall Hopping
- [ ] Whitewater Rafting
- [ ] Sunrise Hike Mount Batur
- [ ] 5am Fishing Trip in Amed
- [ ] Tegalalang Rice Terrace & Giant Swing
- [ ] Balinese Water Ceremony

top 10 *Waterfalls*
TO EXPLORE

- ☐ Suwat
- ☐ Aling Aling
- ☐ Nung Nung
- ☐ Tibumana
- ☐ Sekumpul
- ☐ Kanto Lampo
- ☐ Terjun Kuning
- ☐ Tukad Cupung
- ☐ Leke Leke
- ☐ The Secret Waterfall in Sidemen (you'll have to ask around to discover this adventure)

Things that only happen in *Bali*

YOU KNOW YOU'RE IN BALI WHEN....

01 You post a video every time it rains

02 Your petrol/gas comes in a vodka bottle

03 You're shamed for using a plastic straw

04 You use the word "campur" for everything

05 You follow the @thecanggupole religiously

fun fact!

In the city-areas, Balinese people typically speak 3 languages: Balinese, Indonesian and English.

Bali

THINGS I'M GRATEFUL FOR

_____

_____

_____

_____

_____

psst!

FOR EVERYTHING BALI - FOLLOW
@SOLOGIRLSTRAVELGUIDE ON INSTAGRAM
& YOUTUBE

_____'s

Bali
travel bucket list

00 What's the mission?

▶ *Spend 3 days in Amed*

WHEN? Fall 2021   **WITH WHOM?** Solo!

- THE MASTERPLAN -

To get off-the-beaten tourist path in Amed. I want to slow down, reconnect with nature and spend some time with myself.

PACKING LIST:

* Swimsuits
* A pen + journal
* A mini speaker
* GoPro & Drone
* My Bali Travel Guidebook

MINI GOALS LIST:

* Go on a 5am fishing trip

* Have a beer alone... somewhere

* Spot a sea turtle while snorkeling

* Learn how to Scuba Dive at Abyss

* Swim with plankton in the ocean at night

- COST & BUDGET -

Food - 50 USD
Car Ride from Ubud - 50 USD
3 Nights Accomodation - 75 USD
Open Water Scuba Course - 320 USD

OFFICIALLY TICKED: [X]

DATE COMPLETED: _Spring 2022_   **RATING:** ☆☆☆☆☆

HERE'S THE STORY:
_____
_____
_____
_____
_____
_____
_____

FAVORITE MOMENTS:
Eating dinner & listening to live music at Warung Agung

PEOPLE TO REMEMBER:
Jonathan, my dive instructor

RECOMMENDATIONS & TIPS:
*Try the Chocolate Almond Cake at Rimba Cafe
*Many restaurants offer a free pick-up and drop-off service
*Sleep at Sola Luna Guest House – get the beachfront bungalow

WOULD I DO IT AGAIN? (X) yes ( ) no ( ) maybe

01 What's the mission?

▶ _____

WHEN? _____ WITH WHOM? _____

- THE MASTERPLAN -

PACKING LIST:

MINI GOALS LIST:

- COST & BUDGET -

OFFICIALLY TICKED: ☐

DATE COMPLETED: _____   RATING: ☆☆☆☆☆

HERE'S THE STORY:
_____
_____
_____
_____
_____
_____
_____

FAVORITE MOMENTS:

PEOPLE TO REMEMBER:

RECOMMENDATIONS & TIPS:

WOULD I DO IT AGAIN? ◯ yes   ◯ no   ◯ maybe

02 What's the mission?

▶ _____

WHEN? _____ WITH WHOM? _____

- THE MASTERPLAN -

PACKING LIST:

MINI GOALS LIST:

- COST & BUDGET -

OFFICIALLY TICKED:

DATE COMPLETED: _____ RATING: ☆☆☆☆☆

HERE'S THE STORY:
_____
_____
_____
_____
_____
_____
_____
_____

FAVORITE MOMENTS:

PEOPLE TO REMEMBER:

RECOMMENDATIONS & TIPS:

WOULD I DO IT AGAIN? ◯ yes ◯ no ◯ maybe

03 What's the mission?

▶ _____

WHEN? _____ WITH WHOM? _____

- THE MASTERPLAN -

PACKING LIST:

MINI GOALS LIST:

- COST & BUDGET -

OFFICIALLY TICKED:

DATE COMPLETED: _____ RATING: ☆☆☆☆☆

HERE'S THE STORY:
_____
_____
_____
_____
_____
_____
_____

FAVORITE MOMENTS:	PEOPLE TO REMEMBER:

RECOMMENDATIONS & TIPS:

WOULD I DO IT AGAIN? ◯ *yes* ◯ *no* ◯ *maybe*

01 What's the mission?

▶ _____

WHEN? _____ WITH WHOM? _____

- THE MASTERPLAN -

PACKING LIST:

MINI GOALS LIST:

- COST & BUDGET -

OFFICIALLY TICKED:

DATE COMPLETED: _____   RATING: ☆☆☆☆☆

HERE'S THE STORY:
_____
_____
_____
_____
_____
_____
_____

FAVORITE MOMENTS:

PEOPLE TO REMEMBER:

RECOMMENDATIONS & TIPS:

WOULD I DO IT AGAIN?   ○ yes   ○ no   ○ maybe

05 What's the mission?

▶ _____

WHEN? _____ WITH WHOM? _____

- THE MASTERPLAN -

PACKING LIST:

MINI GOALS LIST:

- COST & BUDGET -

OFFICIALLY TICKED:

DATE COMPLETED: _____   RATING: ☆☆☆☆☆

HERE'S THE STORY:

_____
_____
_____
_____
_____
_____
_____
_____

FAVORITE MOMENTS:

PEOPLE TO REMEMBER:

RECOMMENDATIONS & TIPS:

WOULD I DO IT AGAIN?   ○ *yes*   ○ *no*   ○ *maybe*

06 What's the mission?

▶ _____

WHEN? _____ WITH WHOM? _____

```
- THE MASTERPLAN -
```

PACKING LIST:

MINI GOALS LIST:

- COST & BUDGET -

OFFICIALLY TICKED:

DATE COMPLETED: _____   RATING: ☆☆☆☆☆

HERE'S THE STORY:
_____
_____
_____
_____
_____
_____
_____

FAVORITE MOMENTS:

PEOPLE TO REMEMBER:

RECOMMENDATIONS & TIPS:

WOULD I DO IT AGAIN?   ○ yes   ○ no   ○ maybe

07 What's the mission?

▶ _____

WHEN? _____ WITH WHOM? _____

- THE MASTERPLAN -

PACKING LIST:

MINI GOALS LIST:

- COST & BUDGET -

OFFICIALLY TICKED:

DATE COMPLETED: _____   RATING: ☆☆☆☆☆

HERE'S THE STORY:
_____
_____
_____
_____
_____
_____
_____

FAVORITE MOMENTS:

PEOPLE TO REMEMBER:

RECOMMENDATIONS & TIPS:

WOULD I DO IT AGAIN?   ○ *yes*   ○ *no*   ○ *maybe*

08 What's the mission?

▶ _____

WHEN? _____ WITH WHOM? _____

― THE MASTERPLAN ―

PACKING LIST:

MINI GOALS LIST:

― COST & BUDGET ―

OFFICIALLY TICKED:

DATE COMPLETED: _____   RATING: ☆☆☆☆☆

HERE'S THE STORY:
_____
_____
_____
_____
_____
_____
_____
_____

FAVORITE MOMENTS:

PEOPLE TO REMEMBER:

RECOMMENDATIONS & TIPS:

WOULD I DO IT AGAIN?   ◯ *yes*   ◯ *no*   ◯ *maybe*

09 What's the mission?

▶ _____

WHEN? _____ WITH WHOM? _____

- THE MASTERPLAN -

PACKING LIST:

MINI GOALS LIST:

- COST & BUDGET -

OFFICIALLY TICKED:

DATE COMPLETED: _____   RATING: ☆☆☆☆☆

HERE'S THE STORY:
_____
_____
_____
_____
_____
_____
_____

FAVORITE MOMENTS:	PEOPLE TO REMEMBER:

RECOMMENDATIONS & TIPS:

WOULD I DO IT AGAIN? ◯ *yes*   ◯ *no*   ◯ *maybe*

10 What's the mission?

▶ _____
_____

WHEN? _____ WITH WHOM? _____

- THE MASTERPLAN -

PACKING LIST:

MINI GOALS LIST:

- COST & BUDGET -

OFFICIALLY TICKED:

DATE COMPLETED: _____   RATING: ☆☆☆☆☆

HERE'S THE STORY:
_____
_____
_____
_____
_____
_____
_____

FAVORITE MOMENTS:

PEOPLE TO REMEMBER:

RECOMMENDATIONS & TIPS:

WOULD I DO IT AGAIN?   ◯ *yes*   ◯ *no*   ◯ *maybe*

What's the mission?

▶ _____

WHEN? _____ WITH WHOM? _____

- THE MASTERPLAN -

PACKING LIST:

MINI GOALS LIST:

- COST & BUDGET -

OFFICIALLY TICKED:

DATE COMPLETED: _____ RATING: ☆☆☆☆☆

HERE'S THE STORY:
_____
_____
_____
_____
_____
_____
_____
_____

FAVORITE MOMENTS:	PEOPLE TO REMEMBER:

RECOMMENDATIONS & TIPS:

WOULD I DO IT AGAIN?   ○ yes   ○ no   ○ maybe

12 What's the mission?

▶ _____
_____

WHEN? _____ WITH WHOM? _____

- THE MASTERPLAN -

PACKING LIST:

MINI GOALS LIST:

- COST & BUDGET -

OFFICIALLY TICKED:

DATE COMPLETED: _____   RATING: ☆☆☆☆☆

HERE'S THE STORY:
_____
_____
_____
_____
_____
_____
_____

FAVORITE MOMENTS:

PEOPLE TO REMEMBER:

RECOMMENDATIONS & TIPS:

WOULD I DO IT AGAIN?   ◯ *yes*   ◯ *no*   ◯ *maybe*

13 What's the mission?

▶ _____
_____

WHEN? _____ WITH WHOM? _____

- THE MASTERPLAN -

PACKING LIST:

MINI GOALS LIST:

- COST & BUDGET -

OFFICIALLY TICKED:

DATE COMPLETED: _____   RATING: ☆☆☆☆☆

HERE'S THE STORY:
_____
_____
_____
_____
_____
_____
_____
_____

FAVORITE MOMENTS:

PEOPLE TO REMEMBER:

RECOMMENDATIONS & TIPS:

WOULD I DO IT AGAIN?   ◯ *yes*   ◯ *no*   ◯ *maybe*

124 What's the mission?

▶ _____

WHEN? _____ WITH WHOM? _____

- THE MASTERPLAN -

PACKING LIST:

MINI GOALS LIST:

- COST & BUDGET -

OFFICIALLY TICKED:

DATE COMPLETED: _____   RATING: ☆☆☆☆☆

HERE'S THE STORY:
_____
_____
_____
_____
_____
_____
_____

FAVORITE MOMENTS:

PEOPLE TO REMEMBER:

RECOMMENDATIONS & TIPS:

WOULD I DO IT AGAIN? ○ *yes*   ○ *no*   ○ *maybe*

15 What's the mission?

▶ _____
_____

WHEN? _____ WITH WHOM? _____

- THE MASTERPLAN -

PACKING LIST:

MINI GOALS LIST:

- COST & BUDGET -

OFFICIALLY TICKED:

DATE COMPLETED: _____   RATING: ☆☆☆☆☆

HERE'S THE STORY:
_____
_____
_____
_____
_____
_____
_____

FAVORITE MOMENTS:

PEOPLE TO REMEMBER:

RECOMMENDATIONS & TIPS:

WOULD I DO IT AGAIN?   ○ yes   ○ no   ○ maybe

16 What's the mission?

▶ _____

WHEN? _____ WITH WHOM? _____

- THE MASTERPLAN -

PACKING LIST:

MINI GOALS LIST:

- COST & BUDGET -

OFFICIALLY TICKED:

DATE COMPLETED: _____   RATING: ☆☆☆☆☆

HERE'S THE STORY:

_____
_____
_____
_____
_____
_____
_____
_____

FAVORITE MOMENTS:

PEOPLE TO REMEMBER:

RECOMMENDATIONS & TIPS:

WOULD I DO IT AGAIN?   ◯ yes   ◯ no   ◯ maybe

17 What's the mission?

▶ _____
_____

WHEN? _____ WITH WHOM? _____

- THE MASTERPLAN -

PACKING LIST:

MINI GOALS LIST:

- COST & BUDGET -

OFFICIALLY TICKED:

DATE COMPLETED: _____   RATING: ☆☆☆☆☆

HERE'S THE STORY:

_____
_____
_____
_____
_____
_____
_____
_____

FAVORITE MOMENTS:

PEOPLE TO REMEMBER:

RECOMMENDATIONS & TIPS:

WOULD I DO IT AGAIN?   ◯ *yes*   ◯ *no*   ◯ *maybe*

18 What's the mission?

▶ _____
_____

WHEN? _____ WITH WHOM? _____

- THE MASTERPLAN -

PACKING LIST:

MINI GOALS LIST:

- COST & BUDGET -

OFFICIALLY TICKED:

DATE COMPLETED: _____   RATING: ☆☆☆☆☆

HERE'S THE STORY:
_____
_____
_____
_____
_____
_____
_____
_____

FAVORITE MOMENTS:

PEOPLE TO REMEMBER:

RECOMMENDATIONS & TIPS:

WOULD I DO IT AGAIN?   ○ *yes*   ○ *no*   ○ *maybe*

19 What's the mission?

▶ _____

WHEN? _____ WITH WHOM? _____

- THE MASTERPLAN -

PACKING LIST:

MINI GOALS LIST:

- COST & BUDGET -

OFFICIALLY TICKED:

DATE COMPLETED: _____   RATING: ☆☆☆☆☆

HERE'S THE STORY:
_____
_____
_____
_____
_____
_____
_____
_____

FAVORITE MOMENTS:

PEOPLE TO REMEMBER:

RECOMMENDATIONS & TIPS:

WOULD I DO IT AGAIN? ◯ yes   ◯ no   ◯ maybe

21 What's the mission?

▶ _____

WHEN? _____ WITH WHOM? _____

- THE MASTERPLAN -

PACKING LIST:

MINI GOALS LIST:

- COST & BUDGET -

OFFICIALLY TICKED:

DATE COMPLETED: _____ RATING: ☆☆☆☆☆

HERE'S THE STORY:

_____
_____
_____
_____
_____
_____
_____
_____

FAVORITE MOMENTS:

PEOPLE TO REMEMBER:

RECOMMENDATIONS & TIPS:

WOULD I DO IT AGAIN? ○ yes ○ no ○ maybe

22 What's the mission?

▶ _____

WHEN? _____ WITH WHOM? _____

- THE MASTERPLAN -

PACKING LIST:

MINI GOALS LIST:

- COST & BUDGET -

OFFICIALLY TICKED:

DATE COMPLETED: _____   RATING: ☆☆☆☆☆

HERE'S THE STORY:
_____
_____
_____
_____
_____
_____
_____

FAVORITE MOMENTS:

PEOPLE TO REMEMBER:

RECOMMENDATIONS & TIPS:

WOULD I DO IT AGAIN? ◯ *yes* ◯ *no* ◯ *maybe*

23 What's the mission?

▶ _____

WHEN? _____ WITH WHOM? _____

```
- THE MASTERPLAN -
```

PACKING LIST:

MINI GOALS LIST:

- COST & BUDGET -

OFFICIALLY TICKED:

DATE COMPLETED: _____   RATING: ☆☆☆☆☆

HERE'S THE STORY:
_____
_____
_____
_____
_____
_____
_____
_____

FAVORITE MOMENTS:

PEOPLE TO REMEMBER:

RECOMMENDATIONS & TIPS:

WOULD I DO IT AGAIN?   ◯ *yes*   ◯ *no*   ◯ *maybe*

21 What's the mission?

▶ _____

WHEN? _____ WITH WHOM? _____

- THE MASTERPLAN -

PACKING LIST:

MINI GOALS LIST:

- COST & BUDGET -

OFFICIALLY TICKED:

DATE COMPLETED: _____   RATING: ☆☆☆☆☆

HERE'S THE STORY:
_____
_____
_____
_____
_____
_____
_____

FAVORITE MOMENTS:

PEOPLE TO REMEMBER:

RECOMMENDATIONS & TIPS:

WOULD I DO IT AGAIN?   ○ yes   ○ no   ○ maybe

25 What's the mission?

▶ _____

WHEN? _____ WITH WHOM? _____

- THE MASTERPLAN -

PACKING LIST:

MINI GOALS LIST:

- COST & BUDGET -

OFFICIALLY TICKED:

DATE COMPLETED: _____   RATING: ☆☆☆☆☆

HERE'S THE STORY:
_____
_____
_____
_____
_____
_____
_____
_____

FAVORITE MOMENTS:

PEOPLE TO REMEMBER:

RECOMMENDATIONS & TIPS:

WOULD I DO IT AGAIN?   ◯ *yes*   ◯ *no*   ◯ *maybe*

26 What's the mission?

▶ _____

WHEN? _____ WITH WHOM? _____

- THE MASTERPLAN -

PACKING LIST:

MINI GOALS LIST:

- COST & BUDGET -

OFFICIALLY TICKED:

DATE COMPLETED: _____ RATING: ☆☆☆☆☆

HERE'S THE STORY:
_____
_____
_____
_____
_____
_____
_____

FAVORITE MOMENTS:	PEOPLE TO REMEMBER:

RECOMMENDATIONS & TIPS:

WOULD I DO IT AGAIN? ◯ *yes* ◯ *no* ◯ *maybe*

27 What's the mission?

▶ _____

WHEN? _____ WITH WHOM? _____

- THE MASTERPLAN -

PACKING LIST:

MINI GOALS LIST:

- COST & BUDGET -

OFFICIALLY TICKED:

DATE COMPLETED: _____   RATING: ☆☆☆☆☆

HERE'S THE STORY:

_____
_____
_____
_____
_____
_____
_____
_____

FAVORITE MOMENTS:

PEOPLE TO REMEMBER:

RECOMMENDATIONS & TIPS:

WOULD I DO IT AGAIN?   ◯ *yes*   ◯ *no*   ◯ *maybe*

28 What's the mission?

▶ _____

WHEN? _____ WITH WHOM? _____

- THE MASTERPLAN -

PACKING LIST:

MINI GOALS LIST:

- COST & BUDGET -

OFFICIALLY TICKED:

DATE COMPLETED: _____   RATING: ☆☆☆☆☆

HERE'S THE STORY:
_____
_____
_____
_____
_____
_____
_____

FAVORITE MOMENTS:	PEOPLE TO REMEMBER:

RECOMMENDATIONS & TIPS:

WOULD I DO IT AGAIN?   ○ yes   ○ no   ○ maybe

29 What's the mission?

▶ _____

WHEN? _____ WITH WHOM? _____

- THE MASTERPLAN -

PACKING LIST:

MINI GOALS LIST:

- COST & BUDGET -

OFFICIALLY TICKED:

DATE COMPLETED: _____   RATING: ☆☆☆☆☆

HERE'S THE STORY:
_____
_____
_____
_____
_____
_____
_____
_____

FAVORITE MOMENTS:

PEOPLE TO REMEMBER:

RECOMMENDATIONS & TIPS:

WOULD I DO IT AGAIN?   ◯ yes   ◯ no   ◯ maybe

30 What's the mission?

▶ _____

WHEN? _____ WITH WHOM? _____

- THE MASTERPLAN -

PACKING LIST:

MINI GOALS LIST:

- COST & BUDGET -

OFFICIALLY TICKED:

DATE COMPLETED: _____ RATING: ☆☆☆☆☆

HERE'S THE STORY:
_____
_____
_____
_____
_____
_____
_____
_____

FAVORITE MOMENTS:

PEOPLE TO REMEMBER:

RECOMMENDATIONS & TIPS:

WOULD I DO IT AGAIN? ◯ yes ◯ no ◯ maybe

31 What's the mission?

▶ _____

WHEN? _____ WITH WHOM? _____

- THE MASTERPLAN -

PACKING LIST:

MINI GOALS LIST:

- COST & BUDGET -

OFFICIALLY TICKED:

DATE COMPLETED: _____   RATING: ☆☆☆☆☆

HERE'S THE STORY:
_____
_____
_____
_____
_____
_____
_____

FAVORITE MOMENTS:

PEOPLE TO REMEMBER:

RECOMMENDATIONS & TIPS:

WOULD I DO IT AGAIN?   ◯ *yes*   ◯ *no*   ◯ *maybe*

32 What's the mission?

▶ _____

WHEN? _____ WITH WHOM? _____

- THE MASTERPLAN -

PACKING LIST:

MINI GOALS LIST:

- COST & BUDGET -

OFFICIALLY TICKED:

DATE COMPLETED: _____   RATING: ☆☆☆☆☆

HERE'S THE STORY:
_____
_____
_____
_____
_____
_____
_____
_____

FAVORITE MOMENTS:	PEOPLE TO REMEMBER:

RECOMMENDATIONS & TIPS:

WOULD I DO IT AGAIN? ○ yes ○ no ○ maybe

33 What's the mission?

▶ _____

WHEN? _____ WITH WHOM? _____

- THE MASTERPLAN -

PACKING LIST:

MINI GOALS LIST:

- COST & BUDGET -

OFFICIALLY TICKED:

DATE COMPLETED: _____   RATING: ☆☆☆☆☆

HERE'S THE STORY:
_____
_____
_____
_____
_____
_____
_____
_____

FAVORITE MOMENTS:

PEOPLE TO REMEMBER:

RECOMMENDATIONS & TIPS:

WOULD I DO IT AGAIN?   ○ yes   ○ no   ○ maybe

34 What's the mission?

▶ _____

WHEN? _____ WITH WHOM? _____

- THE MASTERPLAN -

PACKING LIST:

MINI GOALS LIST:

- COST & BUDGET -

OFFICIALLY TICKED:

DATE COMPLETED: _____   RATING: ☆☆☆☆☆

HERE'S THE STORY:
_____
_____
_____
_____
_____
_____
_____
_____

FAVORITE MOMENTS:

PEOPLE TO REMEMBER:

RECOMMENDATIONS & TIPS:

WOULD I DO IT AGAIN?   ◯ yes   ◯ no   ◯ maybe

35 What's the mission?

▶ _____

WHEN? _____ WITH WHOM? _____

- THE MASTERPLAN -

PACKING LIST:

MINI GOALS LIST:

- COST & BUDGET -

OFFICIALLY TICKED:

DATE COMPLETED: _____   RATING: ☆☆☆☆☆

HERE'S THE STORY:
_____
_____
_____
_____
_____
_____
_____
_____

FAVORITE MOMENTS:

PEOPLE TO REMEMBER:

RECOMMENDATIONS & TIPS:

WOULD I DO IT AGAIN?   ○ yes   ○ no   ○ maybe

36 What's the mission?

▶ _____

WHEN? _____ WITH WHOM? _____

- THE MASTERPLAN -

PACKING LIST:

MINI GOALS LIST:

- COST & BUDGET -

OFFICIALLY TICKED:

DATE COMPLETED: _____   RATING: ☆☆☆☆☆

HERE'S THE STORY:
_____
_____
_____
_____
_____
_____
_____

FAVORITE MOMENTS:

PEOPLE TO REMEMBER:

RECOMMENDATIONS & TIPS:

WOULD I DO IT AGAIN?   ◯ *yes*   ◯ *no*   ◯ *maybe*

3 What's the mission?

▶ _____

WHEN? _____ WITH WHOM? _____

- THE MASTERPLAN -

PACKING LIST:

MINI GOALS LIST:

- COST & BUDGET -

OFFICIALLY TICKED:

DATE COMPLETED: _____   RATING: ☆☆☆☆☆

HERE'S THE STORY:
_____
_____
_____
_____
_____
_____
_____
_____

FAVORITE MOMENTS:

PEOPLE TO REMEMBER:

RECOMMENDATIONS & TIPS:

WOULD I DO IT AGAIN?   ◯ yes   ◯ no   ◯ maybe

38 What's the mission?

▶ _____

WHEN? _____ WITH WHOM? _____

- THE MASTERPLAN -

PACKING LIST:

MINI GOALS LIST:

- COST & BUDGET -

OFFICIALLY TICKED:

DATE COMPLETED: _____   RATING: ☆☆☆☆☆

HERE'S THE STORY:
_____
_____
_____
_____
_____
_____
_____
_____

FAVORITE MOMENTS:

PEOPLE TO REMEMBER:

RECOMMENDATIONS & TIPS:

WOULD I DO IT AGAIN?   ◯ yes   ◯ no   ◯ maybe

39 What's the mission?

▶ _____

WHEN? _____ WITH WHOM? _____

- THE MASTERPLAN -

PACKING LIST:

MINI GOALS LIST:

- COST & BUDGET -

OFFICIALLY TICKED:

DATE COMPLETED: _____   RATING: ☆☆☆☆☆

HERE'S THE STORY:
_____
_____
_____
_____
_____
_____
_____
_____

FAVORITE MOMENTS:	PEOPLE TO REMEMBER:

RECOMMENDATIONS & TIPS:

WOULD I DO IT AGAIN?   ◯ yes   ◯ no   ◯ maybe

10 What's the mission?

▶ _____

WHEN? _____ WITH WHOM? _____

- THE MASTERPLAN -

PACKING LIST:

MINI GOALS LIST:

- COST & BUDGET -

OFFICIALLY TICKED:

DATE COMPLETED: _____   RATING: ☆☆☆☆☆

HERE'S THE STORY:
_____
_____
_____
_____
_____
_____
_____

FAVORITE MOMENTS:

PEOPLE TO REMEMBER:

RECOMMENDATIONS & TIPS:

WOULD I DO IT AGAIN? ◯ yes ◯ no ◯ maybe

What's the mission?

▶ _____

WHEN? _____   WITH WHOM? _____

- THE MASTERPLAN -

PACKING LIST:

MINI GOALS LIST:

- COST & BUDGET -

OFFICIALLY TICKED:

DATE COMPLETED: _____ RATING: ☆☆☆☆☆

HERE'S THE STORY:

_____
_____
_____
_____
_____
_____
_____

FAVORITE MOMENTS:

PEOPLE TO REMEMBER:

RECOMMENDATIONS & TIPS:

WOULD I DO IT AGAIN? ◯ *yes* ◯ *no* ◯ *maybe*

12 What's the mission?

▶ _____

WHEN? _____   WITH WHOM? _____

- THE MASTERPLAN -

PACKING LIST:

MINI GOALS LIST:

- COST & BUDGET -

OFFICIALLY TICKED:

DATE COMPLETED: _____   RATING: ☆☆☆☆☆

HERE'S THE STORY:
_____
_____
_____
_____
_____
_____
_____
_____

FAVORITE MOMENTS:

PEOPLE TO REMEMBER:

RECOMMENDATIONS & TIPS:

WOULD I DO IT AGAIN? ○ *yes*   ○ *no*   ○ *maybe*

43 What's the mission?

▶ _____

WHEN? _____ WITH WHOM? _____

- THE MASTERPLAN -

PACKING LIST:

MINI GOALS LIST:

- COST & BUDGET -

OFFICIALLY TICKED:

DATE COMPLETED: _____   RATING: ☆☆☆☆☆

HERE'S THE STORY:
_____
_____
_____
_____
_____
_____
_____

FAVORITE MOMENTS:

PEOPLE TO REMEMBER:

RECOMMENDATIONS & TIPS:

WOULD I DO IT AGAIN?   ◯ yes   ◯ no   ◯ maybe

What's the mission?

▶ _____

WHEN? _____ WITH WHOM? _____

- THE MASTERPLAN -

PACKING LIST:

MINI GOALS LIST:

- COST & BUDGET -

OFFICIALLY TICKED:

DATE COMPLETED: _____   RATING: ☆☆☆☆☆

HERE'S THE STORY:
_____
_____
_____
_____
_____
_____
_____
_____

FAVORITE MOMENTS:

PEOPLE TO REMEMBER:

RECOMMENDATIONS & TIPS:

WOULD I DO IT AGAIN? ◯ *yes* ◯ *no* ◯ *maybe*

45 What's the mission?

▶ _____
_____

WHEN? _____ WITH WHOM? _____

- THE MASTERPLAN -

PACKING LIST:

MINI GOALS LIST:

- COST & BUDGET -

OFFICIALLY TICKED:

DATE COMPLETED: _____ RATING: ☆☆☆☆☆

HERE'S THE STORY:
_____
_____
_____
_____
_____
_____
_____
_____

FAVORITE MOMENTS:

PEOPLE TO REMEMBER:

RECOMMENDATIONS & TIPS:

WOULD I DO IT AGAIN?   ◯ yes   ◯ no   ◯ maybe

16 What's the mission?

▶ _____

WHEN? _____ WITH WHOM? _____

- THE MASTERPLAN -

PACKING LIST:

MINI GOALS LIST:

- COST & BUDGET -

OFFICIALLY TICKED:

DATE COMPLETED: _____   RATING: ☆☆☆☆☆

HERE'S THE STORY:
_____
_____
_____
_____
_____
_____
_____
_____

FAVORITE MOMENTS:

PEOPLE TO REMEMBER:

RECOMMENDATIONS & TIPS:

WOULD I DO IT AGAIN?   ⬤ *yes*   ○ *no*   ○ *maybe*

17 What's the mission?

▶ _____

WHEN? _____ WITH WHOM? _____

- THE MASTERPLAN -

PACKING LIST:

MINI GOALS LIST:

- COST & BUDGET -

OFFICIALLY TICKED:

DATE COMPLETED: _____   RATING: ☆☆☆☆☆

HERE'S THE STORY:

_____
_____
_____
_____
_____
_____
_____

FAVORITE MOMENTS:

PEOPLE TO REMEMBER:

RECOMMENDATIONS & TIPS:

WOULD I DO IT AGAIN?   ○ *yes*   ○ *no*   ○ *maybe*

48 What's the mission?

▶ _____

WHEN? _____ WITH WHOM? _____

- THE MASTERPLAN -

PACKING LIST:

MINI GOALS LIST:

- COST & BUDGET -

OFFICIALLY TICKED:

DATE COMPLETED: _____   RATING: ☆☆☆☆☆

HERE'S THE STORY:

_____
_____
_____
_____
_____
_____
_____

FAVORITE MOMENTS:

PEOPLE TO REMEMBER:

RECOMMENDATIONS & TIPS:

WOULD I DO IT AGAIN?   ◯ *yes*   ◯ *no*   ◯ *maybe*

# **What's the mission?**

▶ _____

WHEN? _____ WITH WHOM? _____

- THE MASTERPLAN -

PACKING LIST:

MINI GOALS LIST:

- COST & BUDGET -

OFFICIALLY TICKED:

DATE COMPLETED: _____ RATING: ☆☆☆☆☆

HERE'S THE STORY:
_____
_____
_____
_____
_____
_____
_____

FAVORITE MOMENTS:

PEOPLE TO REMEMBER:

RECOMMENDATIONS & TIPS:

WOULD I DO IT AGAIN? ◯ yes ◯ no ◯ maybe

50 What's the mission?

▶ _____

WHEN? _____ WITH WHOM? _____

- THE MASTERPLAN -

PACKING LIST:

MINI GOALS LIST:

- COST & BUDGET -

OFFICIALLY TICKED:

DATE COMPLETED: _____ RATING: ☆☆☆☆☆

HERE'S THE STORY:
_____
_____
_____
_____
_____
_____
_____

FAVORITE MOMENTS:

PEOPLE TO REMEMBER:

RECOMMENDATIONS & TIPS:

WOULD I DO IT AGAIN? ◯ *yes* ◯ *no* ◯ *maybe*

00 What's the mission?

▶ _____

WHEN? _____ WITH WHOM? _____

- THE MASTERPLAN -

PACKING LIST:

MINI GOALS LIST:

- COST & BUDGET -

OFFICIALLY TICKED:

DATE COMPLETED: _____   RATING: ☆☆☆☆☆

HERE'S THE STORY:

_____
_____
_____
_____
_____
_____
_____

FAVORITE MOMENTS:

PEOPLE TO REMEMBER:

RECOMMENDATIONS & TIPS:

WOULD I DO IT AGAIN? ○ *yes* ○ *no* ○ *maybe*

Calendar Goals!

__/__/__	__/__/__
__/__/__	__/__/__
__/__/__	__/__/__

where are you going...

...and when?

__/__/__	__/__/__
__/__/__	__/__/__
__/__/__	__/__/__

hey!

Have something to add to the list? Message us at hello@thesologirlstravelguide.com

Travel Hall of Fame!

I'LL NEVER FORGET...

MY FAVORITE HOTEL...

THE FRIENDLIEST PEOPLE...

THE MOST DELICIOUS FOOD...

THE SCARIEST EXPERIENCE...

THE MOST AWKWARD SITUATION...

WHAT I MUST DO AGAIN...

MY FAVORITE PERSON I MET...

THE MOST VALUABLE LESSON I LEARNED...

BEST BALI FASHION ACCESORY..

WEIRDEST BALI TREND...

The best adventures start with the simple decision —*to go!*

travel notes

travel notes

travel notes

travel notes

travel notes

Bali travel challenge!

Take a photo with your journal at your favorite Travel Bucket List Spot.

Tag us for a chance to be featured!

@SoloGirlsTravelGuide
#SOLOGIRLSTRAVEL

DRAW YOUR FAVORITE SPOT!

hey!

Want more bucket list adventures & travel guide books for girls?
Check out TheSoloGirl'sTravelGuide.com

We're a small business run by a badass squad of solo travel women – and your review helps us empower more women to travel the world solo.

Send us a screenshot of your Amazon review - and we'll send you a gift to say 'thank you'

✉ hello@thesologirlstravelguide.com

xoxo

alexa west

+ TRAVEL SQUAD

www.ingramcontent.com/pod-product-compliance
Lightning Source LLC
Chambersburg PA
CBHW071856160426
43209CB00005B/1077